Echoes Of Empty Spaces

R.V. Shloka Rao

BookLeaf Publishing

India | USA | UK

Presentation by *BookLeaf Publishing*

Web: www.bookleafpub.com

E-mail: info@bookleafpub.com

ISBN:9789363311688

First edition 2024

*I dedicate this book to everyone who has
supported me through the journey of writing
this book.*

ACKNOWLEDGEMENT

I would like to thank my parents for giving me the opportunity to write this book.
It has been a dream of mine to write my book of poetry and share it with the world. Those who have bought the book, thank you for making my dream come true.

PREFACE

Most of the poems come straight from my heart and vibrate the feelings of a young teen. It pulsates the emotions in many ways, and I hope it carries you to my world.

Echoes Of My Day

Running through the fields so wide,
Chasing dreams we never hide.
Sunsets paint the sky so bright,
Ending perfect days with light.

Climbing trees and scraping knees,
Laughing loud in the summer breeze.
Secrets shared with whispered glee,
Underneath our favorite tree.

Bike rides to the candy store,
Begging Mom for "Just one more!"
Sticky hands and smiles so sweet,
Counting days for when we meet.

Building forts from sheets and chairs,
Pretending we're in dragon lairs.
Every day a new adventure,
In our world of purest wonder.

Wishing on the evening star,
Wondering if we'll go far.
Innocence and carefree days,
Lost in endless pretend plays.

Memories like treasured gold,
Stories that will never get old.
In our hearts, they'll always stay,
Are echoes of my day.

The Movie Of Life

Life's like a movie, wild and free,
With scenes unfolding, just for me.
I'm the lead in this epic show,
With every day, new places to go.

Wake up each morning, a brand-new scene,
Adventures waiting, big and keen.
School's the backdrop, friends by my side,
Laughter and secrets we never hide.

Months of summer, bikes and sun,
Playing till evening, having fun.
Autumn unfolds with chapters anew,
Leaves that dance, and dreams come true.

Fast-forward moments, birthdays, and more,
Parties and sleepovers, life's never a bore.
Pause for the hard days, tears might flow,
But even heroes have moments of low.

My head filled with future dreams,
Of what I'll be, where the world meets.

Rewind to memories, family times,
Holidays, hugs, silly rhymes.

Soundtrack of laughter, sometimes a fight,
But every scene ends up alright.
Costumes of style, changing with trends,
Plot twists involving best friends.

A Cry In The Dark

In the dark, alone I sit,
Feeling like I don't quite fit.
Tears fall down, they never stop,
Wishing the pain would just drop.
My heart is heavy, eyes so sore,
Can't take this hurt, no more.

Friends are there but far away,
Lonely skies are always gray.
Smile is fake, laugh is gone,
How do I keep holding on?

Dreams are broken, hopes are too,
In this world, what can I do?
Empty room, a silent cry,
Why does it feel like I can't fight?

Every day, the same old fight,
Trying to find a little light.
But darkness wins, it's way too strong,
It's taken way too long.

Melodies Of Emotions

Feelings are like autumn leaves,
Following like the breeze.
Joy and sorrow, love and fear,
Echoes of the heart, so clear.

Happiness, a burst of sun,
Laughing, playing, having fun.
In its warmth, we find our light,
Shining brightly, day and night.

Sadness comes, a gentle rain,
Washing over all the pain.
Tears that fall, a silent please,
Healing hearts so tenderly.

Anger roars, a stormy sea,
Wild and fierce, it sets us free.
Thunder crashes, lightning's spark,
Cleansing fire within the dark.

Love, a flower, soft and sweet,
Binding souls when they meet.
In its bloom, we find our way,
Guiding us through night and day.

Fear, a shadow, cold and tight,
Hiding from the morning light.
Yet in facing what we dread,
Strength and courage move ahead.
Feelings are colours where,
We find the canvas of our life.

Rhythm of Heartbeats

In a world where sunshine meets rain,
Where joy and sorrow dance the same,
I find a place both bright and grey,
Where laughter and tears share the day.

On summer days, with skies so blue,
I play with friends the whole day through.
We chase the wind, we climb so high,
Our life soars, we touch the sky.

But then there are the times alone,
When shadows appear and hope has blown.
I sit and think of what's been lost,
Of friends having fun, the paths they've crossed.

The golden sunsets in the west,
A dazzling ball, a time for rest.
And as it sinks, the colours blend,
A mix of joy and sadness, the day has come to
an end.

Life's a book with pages bright,
With tales of morning, noon, and night.
Some pages filled with endless cheer,
And others marked by silent tears.

So here I stand, at the middle door,
With open heart, I crave for more.
For in this mix of sad and sweet,
I find the rhythm of my heartbeat.

Battlegrounds

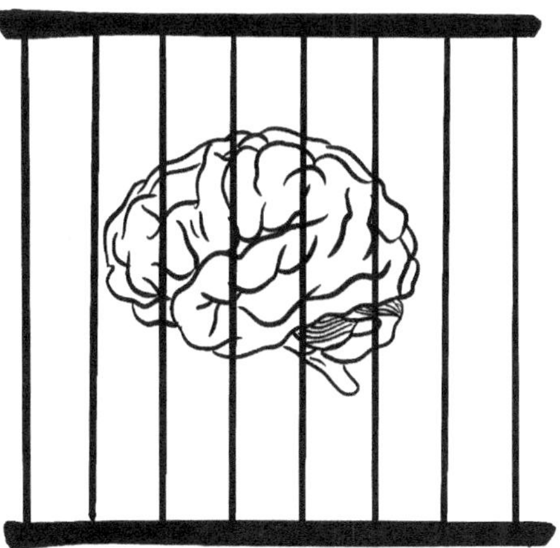

In the battlefield of life, I stand,
A soldier with no sword in hand,
Against the winds of fate, I fight,
In shadows deep, in blinding light.

Midnight breaks with a clear call,
Another day, another fall,
I take the courage and fall in line,
I wonder if it'll all be fine.

Each step I take, a silent war,
With bruises from battles before,
The doubts, they march in a tight formation,
Against my wish, my determination.

The nights are long, the darkness thick,
The moments pass, both slow and quick,
But in the quiet, strength is born,
A fierce response, a soul is made reborn.

For every tear, a drop of rain,
To cleanse the wounds, to ease the pain,
And with each dawn, a brand new start,
A battle won within my heart.

So in this war with life, I stand,
With dreams as weapons in my hand,
For though the fight may never cease,
I'll push ahead and find my peace.

Moonbeams

Stars above, a twinkling choir,
Their melody, a soft desire,
Echoes of dreams that softly sway,
In the stillness of night's display.

Moonbeams cast their gentle light,
Guiding souls through the velvet night,
Mysteries unfold in the dark,
As midnight leaves its subtle mark.

Beneath the moon's enchanting sky,
Where time stands still and dreams take flight,
In the mystic realm of midnight's might.

The night feels like a magic spell,
Where secrets and adventures tell,
Whispers of the night's embrace,
Bring dreams to every quiet place.

Fireflies dance with glowing beams,
Adding sparkle to our dreams,
The world sleeps in silver hue,
As stars share stories, old and new.

So here I stand, beneath the sky,
With dreams as vast as space so high,
In this world of midnight's grace,
I find peace in this quiet place.

Dreams in the Night

In the night so dark and deep,
I lie awake, can't fall asleep.
Stars twinkle in the sky so high,
Whispering secrets as they pass by.

Dreams dance around inside my head,
Like butterflies in gardens spread.
I chase them with eyes closed tight,
Hoping they'll take me on a flight.

Through galaxies and endless space,
Where time slows down, and there's no race.
Where unicorns roam and dragons soar,
And magic fills every hidden door.

In my bed, I start to sway,
Hoping for a dream to come my way.
With each blink, I hope to see,
A world where I can just be me.

In this land where dreams come true,
I'll ride dragons, and the skies won't be blue.
Animals can talk, chocolate flows,
As I go on a journey where no one knows.
No need for worries, no need for fear,
Just laughter and joy, so crystal clear.
In my dreams, I'll find my place,
A world of wonder, a magical space.

Midnight's Tale

In my room, I lay awake,
Thinking of the dreams I want to make.
The stars outside, they seem to gleam,
Telling me to follow my dream.

I wonder what the night will bring,
As I listen to the crickets sing.
In the silence, I hear it call,
The magic of midnight, overall.

I'm not sure what I'll find out there,
In midnight's hush, when all is still,
A whispering breeze, a window sill.
With dreams that dance in silver light,
And shadows waltz through the night.

At thirteen years, I ponder deep,
The mysteries of night, the secrets it keeps.
With heart wide open and secrets glow,
I seek the truths that only midnight knows.

But I'm ready to go, I'm not scared,
With every breath, I take it slow,
Exploring the secrets that only night can show.

So here I am, at thirteen years old,
Ready to step into the stories untold.
With wonder in my heart and stars above,
I'll embrace the magic of midnight, a silent cove.

Classroom Chronicles

In the land of studies and fun,
Where friendships spark and where we run.
School days are like a rollercoaster ride,
With heights of laughter, we can't hide.

First period's math, a maze to solve,
Algebra's a puzzle, but I'll evolve.
English class next, where stories unfold,
Imagination flies in tales untold.

Lunchtime chaos, a cafeteria brawl,
Trading snacks and jokes, having a ball.
Then it's science time, experiments in sight,
Mixing potions, chasing sparks of light.

History class, where the past comes alive,
Stories of triumph, stories of strive.
And finally, the bell rings loud and clear,
Homework awaits, but freedom is near.

School days end in a colorful blend,
With memories made that will never end.
Through ups and downs, we'll find our way,
In the adventure of life, day by day.

Journey Of Life

Life's a journey, that's what they say,
And here I am, finding my way.
With my backpack filled with dreams so bright,
I set out alone, from morning till night.

Each day's a road, unknown and new,
With ups and downs and skies so blue.
I walk alone, but I don't mind,
For every step, a surprise to find.

Friends wave goodbye, "See you soon!"
As I chase the sun and follow the moon.
The path is mine, to laugh and roam,
To find my place, my heart's true home.

Sometimes I trip, and sometimes I fall,
But I get back up, standing tall.
For life's a maze, a winding quest,
With each twist and turn, I try my best.

Trees whisper secrets, rivers sing songs,
I learn from nature, righting wrongs.
Birds fly high, showing the way,
Teaching me to hope every single day.

I meet new faces, kind and sweet,
Share stories and smiles with everyone I meet.
Each person's journey, a tale to tell,
In this big world, we all fit well.

So here I go, step by step,
With dreams and courage, no need to fret.
Life's a journey, and I'm on my own,
But I'll find my way, my heart's true home.

Fall And Rise

I thought I knew it all, so strong,
But then I found I could be wrong.
The world's a place where we can trip,
And learn some lessons from each slip.

I tried to build the tallest tower,
But then it fell within an hour.
I learned that things can fall apart,
And sometimes you need a fresh start.

I took a test and did my best,
But still, I failed like all the rest.
I learned that effort doesn't always show,
And that's a lesson I now know.

I trusted someone with my secret small,
But soon enough, they told it all.
I learned that trust is something rare,
And not everyone will care.

I joined a game, I thought I'd win,
But others played better, with a grin.
I learned that losing isn't bad,
It's just a chance to not be sad.

I made a mess, I spilled my drink,
And had to clean it in a blink.
I learned that fixing what you break,
Is something that you have to take.

These lessons hurt, they made me see,
The world is big and not all free.
But now I know, and that's okay,
I'm learning more with each new day.

Adventure Awaits

Packing bags, feeling excited,
New adventures, so delighted.
Maps and plans, where shall we go?
The world is big, with lots to show!

Airplanes zooming, high in the sky,
Clouds like marshmallows passing by.
Peering out the tiny window,
Watching cities far below.

Train tracks clack, clickety-clack,
Through valleys green and mountains black.
Scenery changing, mile by mile,
Every view makes me smile.

In the car, on winding roads,
With family, sharing loads.
Singing songs and playing games,
Traveling isn't always the same.

New places, new faces, new things to try,
From sandy beaches to mountains high.
Every journey, a story to tell,
In my heart, these memories dwell.

So let's keep exploring, near and far,
By plane, by train, by car.
Traveling the world, young and free,
Every adventure, a part of me.

Knights And Dragons

In a land of castles tall,
Where shadows of the dragons fall,
Brave knights ride with swords held high,
Against the beasts that fill the sky.

The dragons breathe their fiery breath,
A roar that echoes tales of death.
But knights, with armor shining bright,
Stand firm and ready for the fight.

With banners waving in the air,
They charge ahead without a care.
Their hearts are filled with courage, true,
To save the land, that's what they'll do.

The dragons' eyes, a burning glow,
But knights have strength, they seldom show.
They fight for honor, fight for peace,
And dream of when the wars will cease.

In the darkest caves, where dragons sleep,
Where secrets ancient shadows keep,
Knights venture forth with silent steps,
To face the terror, no regrets.

And when the battle's finally won,
And dragons fall with the setting sun,
The knights return with tales to tell,
Of battles fierce where dragons fell.

Yet in their eyes, a sorrow deep,
For dragons too, must dreams keep.
They wonder if there's another way,
Where knights and dragons, friends, could stay.

In a world of black and white,
Where wrong and right are often tight,
Maybe there's a land unknown,
Where peace and friendship could be shown.

For now, the knights will guard the realm,
With bravery, they take the helm.
But in their hearts, they hold a dream,
Of a world where dragons aren't so mean.

Night's Gaze

In the quiet hours when the moonlight fades,
Whispers of sorrow in a somber parade,
A shadow walks in the depths of my mind,
A sad tune only the heart can find.

Tears like rain fall from weary eyes,
In the vast expanse of night's dark skies,
Each drop, a story of longing and pain,
My life drifts on waves of sadness strain.

The echoes of laughter, now distant and faint,
Now buried deep in a regretful sprain,
Ghosts of joy that once brightly burned,
Lessons of hate painfully learned.

But in this darkness, a fragile light gleams,
For even in sadness, there are dreams,
A hope that sorrow is not forever,
That someday hearts will mend and serve.

Happiness.

In the morning light, golden and bright,
Each moment fills with pure delight,
A symphony of joy fills the air,
A dance of laughter, free from care.

The world is in bloom, vibrant and alive,
Every breath, a thrill to thrive,
Colors of joy paint the sky,
Under the sun's watchful eye.

Eyes twinkle with a joyous fire,
In this moment, all desires,
A heart that soars on wings of bliss,
Fulfilled in the warmth of coca cola fizz.

Oh, happiness, a flying guest,
In your presence, we are blessed,
Yet cherished with each beat,
Life's every regret happily beat.

Fragments Of Heart

My heart feels like it's shattered glass,
Broken pieces, sharp and will never last.
It used to beat with joy and love,
But now it feels like it's been shoved.

I gave my love, I gave my trust,
But now it feels like it's just dust.
Promises made but never kept,
Leaving me alone, feeling wrecked.

I thought we'd be together forever,
But now I'm lost, without a tether.
The pain inside, it feels so real,
Like an open wound that will never heal.

I'll pick up the pieces, one by one,
And slowly, surely, I'll find the sun.
Though my heart may be broken and sore,
I'll learn to love myself even more.

For even broken hearts can mend,
And one day, my sadness will end.
I'll be stronger than I was before,
With a heart that's broken but still pure.

Time Flies

In the attic, dusty and old,
I found a box, its secrets untold.
Inside were treasures from years ago,
Memories forgotten, hidden in a shadow.

I remember the day I climbed up high,
Through cobwebs and shadows, reaching for the
sky.
The box was waiting, covered in dust,
But inside was a treasure box with rust.

Photos of smiles and laughter so bright,
Letters and cards, memories come alive.
Toys from childhood, put away,
But in that moment, they all came to play.

Each item, a story, a piece of my past,
A journey through time, too precious to last.
In the attic, dusty and old,
I found a box worth more than gold.

Life And Space

Life is like a rocket, soaring high,
With stars and planets in the sky.
It's full of wonder, big and vast,
Moments that fly by, oh so fast.

Space is like a mystery, waiting to explore,
With galaxies and comets, so much more.
It's like a puzzle waiting to be solved,
With secrets hidden, yet to be evolved.

Life is like a shooting star, blazing bright,
Leaving trails of magic in the night.
It's filled with dreams, ready to chase,
And memories to cherish in every embrace.

Space is like a canvas, wide and grand,
Painted with stars by a celestial hand.
It's a reminder of how small we are,
In this universe, a shining star.

A Canvas Of Tears

If my tears were colored, what hues they'd
impart,
Each drop, a story, a piece of my heart.
Upon my pillow, they'd paint a tale,
Of joys and sorrows, that'll never pale.

In shades of blue, they'd softly weep,
A river of emotions, vast and deep.
A canvas of grief, yet beauty unfolds,
In every teardrop, a story told.

In gentle greens, they'd speak of peace,
Moments of calm that never cease.
While yellows shine on sunny days,
And laughter's warmth in golden rays.

In reds, they'd burn with anger's flame,
Yet even this has no shame.
For every hue and every tone,
Reveals a part of me alone.

So let them fall, these tears of mine,
In colors rich, in shades divine.
For on my pillow, they find release,
Creating beauty in sadness, a masterpiece.

The Breath Of Happiness

I hope that God makes the air you inhale happy,
So every breath feels light and snappy.
With every puff and every sigh,
May joy be found in the sky.

I wish for giggles in the breeze,
And smiles to float among the trees.
Let laughter swirl with every gust,
And happiness be a must.

When you breathe in, feel the cheer,
Know that happiness is near.
In every breath, both day and night,
May your heart feel pure delight.

So take a breath and close your eyes,
Imagine joy that never dies.
I hope that God makes the air you inhale happy,
To fill your days with sunshine, snappy.